Great Jobs in
Sports

Heidi C. Feldman

San Diego, CA

About the Author

Heidi C. Feldman is an author, editor, and educator. Her book about Afro-Peruvian music won the Woody Guthrie Book Prize from the International Association of Popular Music (US) and was published in Spanish translation in Peru. She was a volume editor for *Bloomsbury Encyclopedia of Popular Music of the World*. She has taught at San Diego State University, University of California–San Diego, Soka University of America, and Tulane University. She lives in San Diego with her family.

For more information, contact:
ReferencePoint Press, Inc.
PO Box 27779
San Diego, CA 92198
www.ReferencePointPress.com

Picture Credits:

Cover: Kali9/iStockphoto.com
 6: Maury Aaseng
11: Aspen Photo/Shutterstock.com
20: digitalskillet/Shutterstock.com
29: Brian Cahn/Zuma Press/Newscom
37: Steve Debebport/iStockphoto.com
61: ESB Professional/Shutterstock.com

LIBRARY OF CONGRESS CATALOGING-IN-PUBLICATION DATA

Names: Feldman, Heidi Carolyn, 1965– author.
Title: Great Jobs in Sports/by Heidi C. Feldman.
Description: San Diego, CA: ReferencePoint Press, Inc., [2019] | Series:
 Great jobs | Includes bibliographical references and index. | Audience:
 Grade 9 to 12.
Identifiers: LCCN 2018031463 (print) | LCCN 2018034017 (ebook) | ISBN
 9781682825280 (eBook) | ISBN 9781682825273 (hardback)
Subjects: LCSH: Sports—Vocational guidance—Juvenile literature.
Classification: LCC GV734.3 (ebook) | LCC GV734.3 .F45 2019 (print) | DDC
 796.023—dc23
LC record available at https://lccn.loc.gov/2018031463

Contents

Dream Jobs in a Growing and Changing Industry

In a 2015 nationwide survey, five hundred children aged ten and under told the parenting digital media site Fatherly what they wanted to be when they grew up. The number one choice for boys was professional athlete. The top choice for girls was doctor. Both professions, in fact, are possible jobs in sports.

For many adults, both male and female, working in sports is a dream job. The range of opportunities for sports professionals includes employment in a growing number of fields with specializations related to sports (including sports doctors, sportswriters, coaches, and more). According to Glenn Wong, author of *The Comprehensive Guide to Careers in Sports*, many people are drawn to jobs in sports because of the sense of magic and excitement. Wong writes, "In talking to many people who currently work in the sports industry, it is typical to find very high rates of job satisfaction." In fact, many sports professionals are quoted in the media saying they have the best job in the world. Perhaps job satisfaction is one of the reasons that there is such high demand for jobs in sports.

An Industry in Flux

While there is intense competition for most jobs in sports, the sports industry is growing. The North American sports market (including media rights, ticket sales, sponsorships, and merchandising), valued at $60.5 billion in 2014, is projected to reach $78.5

billion by 2021, according to the forecasting report PwC Sports Outlook. The PwC findings continue an earlier trend reported by CareerBuilder and Economic Modeling Specialists Intl., which found that job growth of 12.6 percent in the six largest US sports-related industries from 2010 to 2014 outpaced the overall US job market growth of 5.5 percent. In addition, a study by WinterGreen Research, published in *Time* in 2017, found that the youth sports economy had grown by 55 percent since 2010 and was valued at $15.3 billion. Finally, according to the Bureau of Labor Statistics, participation in college and women's sports is expected to increase over the next ten years, signaling one of the ways in which social changes in the industry may create future job opportunities.

Along with financial growth and expansion, the sports industry is moving in significant new directions that shape the job market. These include breakthroughs for women, increased awareness of safety and health concerns, and the transformative impact of emerging technology.

In a 2016 article on the website of business magazine *Inc.*, tech entrepreneur Mandy Antoniacci writes that one of the "game-changing trends" in the sports industry is the emerging importance of women's participation. In 2015 the Women's World Cup final was the most-watched soccer match in US history. That same year Sarah Thomas became the NFL's first female referee. In 2016, *Sports Illustrated* renamed its "Sportsman of the Year" award to Sportsperson of the Year and conferred that honor on tennis player Serena Williams. Also that year, former Olympic softball player Jessica Mendoza made history on ESPN as the first female announcer to broadcast a nationally televised MLB postseason game. As women break into a long male-dominated industry, more young girls may choose professional athlete or other sports-related jobs as what they want to be when they grow up.

Transformation and Opportunity

Increased understanding of the relationship between sports and physical and mental health is also likely to impact future

Great Jobs in Sports

Occupation	Minimum Educational Requirement	2017 Median Pay
Athletic trainer	Bachelor's degree	$46,630
Coach and scout	Bachelor's degree	$32,270
Dietitian and nutritionist	Bachelor's degree	$59,410
Fitness trainer and instructor	High school diploma or equivalent	$39,210
Phyiscal therapist	Doctoral or professional degree	$86,850
Physical therapist assistant and aide	Associate's degree for assistants; high school diploma or equivalent for aides	$46,920
Public relations specialist	Bachelor's degree	$59,300
Recreation worker	High school diploma or equivalent	$24,540
Stastician	Master's degree	$84,760
Umpire, referee, and other sports official	High school diploma or equivalent	$26,800

Source: Bureau of Labor Statistics, *Occupational Outlook Handbook*, 2018. www.bls.gov.

employment in sports. For example, studies have documented the role of concussions in contributing to long-term behavioral and cognitive problems, depression, and the brain disease chronic traumatic encephalopathy. As the NFL, schools, and youth sports organizations strive to prevent concussions and other debilitating injuries, new opportunities exist for jobs in research, education, and preventive technology and training. In addition, increasing recognition of the importance of mental health and mental preparation in sports has contributed to the recent rise of sport psychology.

Finally, technology has transformed professions throughout the sports industry. Sports journalism, for example, has moved away from the dominance of print media to fully embrace social media and Internet publications. Sports broadcasters work with sophisticated television production technologies, including the use of drones, remote production and production automation, and virtual and augmented reality techniques. These technological advances have enhanced the popularity and experience of sports television for home viewing audiences, and they have created jobs. An entirely new technology-based activity that only recently gained recognition as a sport is eSports (electronic sports). These competitive video games, played in live contests that employ programmers, hosts, players, venue managers, and other professionals, are now part of the varsity athletics program at several US universities and are covered on television networks. According to Antoniacci, "eSports is not only exploding, but it's poised to become the most popular sport in the 21st century." As new sports and sports technologies emerge, then, so do new jobs in sports.

Athlete

When competitive swimmer Michael Phelps was eight years old, he wrote his goals in red pen on a sheet of paper. Phelps's goals, which appear in a 2015 article on the NBC Sports website, included "I would like to make the Olympics" and "I would like to make Jr. in at least one event." He also wrote an action plan: "I will accomplish these goals by concentrating hard, working hard, and coming to every practice."

Phelps achieved, and surpassed, his goals. He grew up to become not only a professional athlete but also the most decorated Olympian athlete (as of 2018), winning twenty-eight Olympic medals over the course of his career. Many young athletes share Phelps's dream, but only a few achieve it. There is intense competition for the small number of positions available for athletes in professional sports. Those who do become professional athletes may be guaranteed that—like Phelps—they will have to concentrate hard, work hard, and practice hard.

The day-to-day work of most professional athletes consists primarily of preparing for and playing in sports competitions. Athletes

At a Glance

Athlete

Minimum Educational Requirements
No formal education credential required

Personal Qualities
Physical strength, stamina, dedication

Certification and Licensing
Required for a few types of athletes in most states

Working Conditions
Indoors and outdoors, extreme weather, high risk of injury

Salary Range
About $19,220 to millions of dollars

Number of Jobs
About 11,800 in 2016

Future Job Outlook
About average job growth

must spend many hours every day practicing, training, and exercising to maintain and improve their skills, physical and mental strength, and agility. Before he retired, Phelps, for example, told NBC reporters in a 2016 interview that he spent twenty-five to thirty hours each week in physical training, including three or more days of weight lifting. He also worked with his coach on mental training exercises, including visualizing success. Training is necessary not only to promote strength but also to prevent injury. Early in her career, Megan Rapinoe, a star soccer player for Seattle Reign FC in the National Women's Soccer League, learned the importance of effective daily preventive training after she tore her anterior cruciate ligament (ACL) twice. Rapinoe reflects in the sports magazine *Stack*, "I think it helped me grow and learn how to take care of my body. . . . Training is not just about getting stronger and faster. It's about injury prevention." Rapinoe now uses specialized exercises and self-massage to keep her muscles and body in good working condition.

In addition, athletes often follow rigorous dietary or nutritional programs (sometimes prescribed by a nutritionist and sometimes self-directed) to ensure maximum performance in their chosen sport. Tennis pro Serena Williams, for example, eats a mostly raw diet and tries to avoid wheat. Ultramarathon athlete Scott Jurek prepares for long-distance runs by eating a vegan, plant-based diet. World champion climber Sasha DiGiulian eats six protein- and carbohydrate-heavy meals a day.

Specific approaches to training, nutrition, and other aspects of an athlete's daily regimen vary depending on the particular sport. Some of the professional team sports that employ athletes include football, baseball, soccer, basketball, hockey, and rugby. Athletes also compete in individual sports such as tennis, golf, martial arts, swimming, gymnastics, and skiing. Many of these sports are officiated by professional umpires, judges, or referees and are performed for a spectator audience. Some athletes may also perform in solo exhibitions of their skills.

Athletes interact with many types of people. They are usually supervised at regular individual and group practice sessions by coaches, who instruct them on strategy, tactics, and teamwork. Many athletes work with a trainer to develop their strength and capacity and to learn how to prevent injuries. Travel may be required for games and athletic events. At games, athletes must not only perform physically but also understand rules and execute strategies. They must follow directions from coaches and officials. After games and events, athletes work with their coaches and teammates to evaluate recent performance and prepare for upcoming events. Some athletes participate in promotional activities, such as interviews and events involving fans and the media.

How Do You Become an Athlete?

Education

Becoming an athlete does not require an educational degree or credential. However, athletes must know the rules of their sport inside and out, and they must have learned and practiced playing techniques and strategies. Professional athletes develop skills and visibility by playing on their school-sponsored teams at the high school and college levels. Many sports agents and scouts recruit new players by keeping an eye on rising talent in high school, college, and club sports teams. In some sports, professional players are recruited directly from college teams. This is the case in football, for example, so athletes who would like to play for the NFL should plan to attend college. In contrast, professional baseball teams recruit from the minor league teams, and players may enter the draft immediately after high school.

Certification and Licensing

A few amateur and professional sports, such as boxing, wrestling, and martial arts, sometimes require certificates or licenses, handled at the state level. Applicants usually submit evidence of a recent medical examination and clearance proving that they are physically able to compete.

Getting Experience

Future pro athletes often gain experience through participation in recreational, club, and school-sponsored sports teams. However,

College basketball players showcase their talents. In some sports, such as professional basketball and football, players are typically recruited from college teams.

the American Academy of Pediatrics recommends that young people play different sports each season. Many studies have shown that when children play one sport all year, they are more prone to injury and burnout. Coaches and recruiters also back this advice. For example, Seattle Seahawks football coach and former University of Southern California (USC) coach Pete Carroll affirms that he looks for broad sports experience when he recruits an athlete. In an interview with USC quarterback Sam Darnold, available on the 2017 USC podcast *Season of Sam*, Carroll states:

> I've always discouraged parents from keeping their kid from playing other sports and encouraged them to let them play everything. I don't know this about you, Sam, but I bet you can shoot a hoop, and I bet you can hit a golf ball, and I bet you were a shortstop and a pitcher, and all of that growing up. And you were probably the "go to guy" in 7th and 8th grade, in basketball, and probably could have been in high school, if you were not already. You needed to be all of those things to be the athlete that can make the decisions in this unbelievably tasking position of quarterback in football.

Skills and Personality

The US Department of Labor's Bureau of Labor Statistics (BLS) lists the following skills and personality traits of professional athletes: athleticism, concentration, decision-making skills, dedication, hand-eye coordination, stamina, and teamwork. Character and the ability to rebound from failure are also key. Scouts, for example, look for evidence of potential recruits' character by observing how they handle setbacks. In an excerpt from an interview that appears on the website Baseball America, an anonymous scout explains that character matters a great deal. "These kids, particularly at the high school level, they're all big fish in small ponds. Not a whole lot of them have failed to any significant degree and they're all going to fail in pro ball at some level. Every single guy out there. Every guy, whatever the story is behind them, is going to hit a tough spot and you want to see how he's going to deal with adversity."

Other important qualities include a high level of motivation, interest in physical fitness, and willingness to perform publicly in front of strangers. Athletes must work closely with other people, whether they compete on a team or individually, so they should also be good listeners and communicators.

On the Job

Employers

According to the BLS, over half of professional athletes in 2016 worked in spectator sports. A much smaller percentage of professional athletes are self-employed or work in fitness and recreational sports centers.

Working Conditions

Athletes employed in the spectator sports industry "live" their sport. They may have to work long and irregular hours with little time off, including weekends, holidays, and evenings. It is common for athletes to spend many hours in games and competitions during the playing season, with the rest of the year dedicated to training and preparing for competition. Travel is often required to attend local, national, regional, and international competitions. Relocation may be necessary if a player is traded from one team to another. Athletes may practice and compete either indoors or outdoors, and in some places athletes may have to perform in extreme weather conditions (including rain, snow, or heat). In most sports, there is a significant risk of bodily harm, including fatal injuries. Growing awareness of the dangers of brain injuries from sports-related concussions has led to efforts to improve safety measures for athletes.

Earnings

Some professional athletes earn extremely high salaries. The highest-paid 10 percent earned over $208,000 in 2017, and celebrity athletes earn millions of dollars annually, in part from major endorsement deals with companies. However, astronomically high salaries are not the norm for most athletes. Professional soccer player Christie Rampone, for example, explains on the ESPN website that having her "dream job" with the Sky Blue startup women's soccer league sometimes comes at a financial cost: "In the beginning years of a league there just isn't a lot of money. The minimum salary is something like $6,000 for March through August, so nobody's getting rich here." According to the BLS, in May 2017 professional athletes and sports competitors earned a median wage of $51,370. The lowest-paid 10 percent earned under $19,220 annually.

Opportunities for Advancement

In 2018 an NCAA study found that a very small subset of collegiate athletes is likely to go on to play professionally in sports, including baseball (9.5 percent), basketball (1.2 percent of men and 0.9 percent of women), football (1.6 percent), ice hockey (6.4 percent), and soccer (1.4 percent). With far fewer jobs than athletes hoping to fill them, only the very dedicated and fortunate few are likely to rise to the professional level.

Because an athlete's career longevity depends on continued physical strength and endurance, those who become professional athletes should expect a relatively short and intense period of employment in the field. Some newly signed athletes begin to compete right away, while others remain in reserves or on the bench and hope to advance to a higher level of competition. Advancement may also take the form of moving to higher-ranked teams or levels within a sport (for example, a baseball or ice hockey player may move from a minor league team to a major league team) or from one team to another with newly negotiated contracts that offer higher pay and benefits.

Outstanding performance in competitions enables some athletes to earn pay raises and company endorsements or deals to advertise products. However, some careers end quickly due to injuries or performance below expectations. Therefore, it is advisable for professional athletes to be prepared for a second or fallback career.

What Is the Future Outlook for Athletes?

The BLS estimates average growth in employment of athletes and sports competitors through 2026 at 7 percent. One source of growth may be a projected population increase. The BLS predicts that some sports leagues may expand into cities where teams have not previously existed, creating new jobs.

Find Out More

National Collegiate Athletic Association (NCAA)
700 W. Washington St.
PO Box 6222
Indianapolis, IN 46206
website: www.ncaa.org

The NCAA is a national organization that oversees and regulates college sports championship events, institutions, and conferences and provides scholarships and academic assistance for student athletes. It provides resources and information for current, future, and former college athletes, as well as detailed sections pertaining to each of its three college sports divisions.

National Council of Youth Sports

7185 SE Seagate Lane
Stuart, FL 34997
website: www.ncys.org

The National Council of Youth Sports is a large membership and advocacy organization that represents organized amateur youth sports programs across America. Its website provides information about safety in sports, education (including online coach training and health and wellness links), events and meetings, sports publications, and recent youth sports news.

National Federation of State High School Associations (NFHS)

PO Box 690
Indianapolis, IN 46206
website: www.nfhs.org

The NFHS establishes and disseminates the rules for sixteen sports played in US high schools. Its website contains detailed, up-to-date information about the rules of these sports, as well as sport-specific resources, information for coaches and officiators, an area for student athletes, and a wide range of publications on topics from sports medicine to participation statistics.

US Olympic Committee

1 Olympic Plaza
Colorado Springs, CO 80909
website: www.teamusa.org

The US Olympic Committee, as the national governing body for Olympic sports, manages the US teams for the Olympic Games, Paralympic Games, Youth Olympic Games, Pan American Games, and Parapan American Games. Its website provides information about these competitions and links to US training centers, up-to-date news, and player profiles.

Coach

Tom Houser is a veteran coach who has led top-rated club and school volleyball teams in Virginia since 1985. In an interview posted on Volleyball Training Ground's website, Houser reflects on his job. He explains that he views coaching as an intensely creative—even artistic—profession: "Coaching is like being an artist. If you work hard at it, do the right things, are careful . . . you can create something beautiful. Will it always be a masterpiece? Of course not. But I intend for them, all of my teams, to be masterpieces. And, then, sometimes, the coach and team together can create a once-in-lifetime priceless memory."

Coaches build memories from season to season by guiding and encouraging athletes to play their best and (in team sports) to contribute to a strong and effective team. To work toward these goals on a daily basis, coaches plan and supervise regular practice and training sessions, drills, and physical conditioning exercises, and they lead teamwork initiatives. They implement motivational strategies to encourage teamwork and

At a Glance

Coach

Minimum Educational Requirements
Bachelor's degree is helpful

Personal Qualities
Leadership and communication skills, resilience, quick thinking, resourcefulness

Certification and Licensing
Varies by state, employer type, and sport

Working Conditions
Indoor and outdoor, extreme weather, long and irregular hours, travel

Salary Range
About $18,670 to $11 million or more

Number of Jobs
About 276,100 in 2016 (includes coaches and scouts)

Future Job Outlook
Better than average (includes coaches and scouts)

top individual performances. They know and follow prescribed procedures to keep their players safe.

In addition to promoting physical athleticism, coaches also serve as supportive mentors to individual players. Bela Karolyi, a gymnastics coach whose athletes have won Olympic gold medals, explains in an interview in *Harvard Business Review* that a key to effective coaching is to discover the unique personality and needs of each athlete. "You have to take them individually," he states. "Find out what part of their mind is clicking, what part of their character is responding to you, and what's the one thing you have to avoid. . . . Each time, you have a totally different approach." To guide individual athletes toward maximum performance, coaches keep records of athletes' performance at games and review strengths and weaknesses.

To build a strong team and recruit players, many college coaches scout for talented athletes by visiting high schools across the country. Increasingly, college coaches use social media as a recruiting tool, checking a candidate's Facebook, Twitter, and Instagram pages for character insight. Many coaches run tryouts to decide who will be offered a place on teams and in which positions. In K–12 schools with teams that are open to all students, coaches try to elicit the best possible performance and sportsmanship from athletes of varying skill levels.

Before the season begins, coaches schedule appropriate competitions for their athletes. To prepare athletes for games and events, coaches provide instructions about rules, strategies, techniques, and behavior. Team coaches study and analyze other teams' performance to develop effective strategies to counter their strengths or weaknesses. Similarly, a gymnastics coach may instruct a gymnast to include in his or her routine a skill not likely to be executed by other competing athletes.

At competitions, coaches are constantly "on." They decide which team members will participate in what ways, advise players about situations as they occur, and make last-minute calls, including player substitutions and changes of strategy. As former New York Yankees manager Joe Girardi observes in *Harvard Business Review*, coaches must be ready to make instant decisions: "If you think too much, you fail, because the game happens too quickly. The key is preparation. . . . The data has to become instinctual. You can't think about it in the middle of a pitch."

In addition to teaching athletes the skills they need to succeed, coaches impart sportsmanship skills and resilience. Former NFL quarterback and former head coach of the Grambling State Tigers, Doug Williams, addresses how coaches guide their players to handle both wins and losses in his widely quoted message (part of Bleacher Report's list of most inspirational sports quotes): "Never give up, never give in, and when the upper hand is ours, may we have the ability to handle the win with the dignity that we absorbed the loss." In other words, coaches prepare athletes to win—and lose—with grace.

How Do You Become a Coach?

Education
Degrees are not always required, but they can be helpful. Useful majors include physical education, sports medicine, physiology, kinesiology, and nutrition and fitness.

Coaches must be experts in the skills, rules, and procedures associated with their sport. Most have prior experience as players. For example, triathlon and paratriathlon coach Liesl Begnaud competed in triathlons herself for thirteen years before she started coaching for Team MPI. In an interview with Female Coaching Network, she explains, "I decided that I wanted to share my passion, skills, knowledge and experience with other adults who were looking to attempt their first triathlon. . . . I had been told by numerous other athletes that they thought I would be a great coach and I was driven to connect my racing experience with the specific knowledge of coaching."

Certification and Licensing
Certification requirements for coaching vary by state, employer type, and sport. Several organizations offer coaching certification for specific sports. Coaches in public high schools normally must

be certified in cardiopulmonary resuscitation and first aid, and some states require public high school coaches to have completed courses in sports safety and coaching fundamentals. In addition, since many high school administrators prefer to employ current subject-area teachers or school administrators as coaches, a teaching credential or license is advantageous. Schools may conduct an applicant background check. For coaches who work in youth leagues and small recreational facilities or private schools, certification may or may not be needed.

Volunteer Work and Internships

Southampton Football Club coach Stephen King advises young people who hope to find a coaching job to actively seek out volunteer opportunities. "Gain as much experience as possible," he suggests in an interview published on the Bright Knowledge website. "This may involve a lot of unpaid volunteering work, working with and learning from other coaches with different qualifications who work with different ages and abilities. You need to be patient, as you will not go from a new coach to a professional coach overnight."

Some coaches gain volunteer experience as graduate assistants before seeking professional employment. There are also opportunities to volunteer as assistant coaches for recreational sports and in community settings such as Little League Baseball or summer camps.

Skills and Personality

In order to motivate and inspire athletes, coaches must be effective communicators and teachers, with excellent interpersonal and leadership skills. Most coaches work with young athletes during their career, even if they go on to coach adults. Volleyball coach Anne Kordes explains that school coaches will find job fulfillment if they enjoy working with children: "It's not all about trophies and honors. What makes me proud is mentoring and caring for my kids."

Effective coaching of both children and adults includes more than teaching skills and techniques. Renowned football coach Bill Walsh was known for his view that a coach's job is similar to that of the business manager of a company. He explains in an

Coaches plan and supervise training, practice, and physical conditioning. They also mentor athletes, plan game day strategies, and mold individual players into a team that works together.

interview with *Harvard Business Review*, "In coaching, I think of it as the coach's ability to condition the athletes' minds and to train them to think as a unit, while at the same time, making sure each athlete approaches his own game with total concentration, intensity, and skill." In addition to being good managers, coaches must be effective problem solvers. They should be resourceful and creative enough to analyze a competitive situation and devise a plan for winning. Finally, since there is a winner and a loser in most sports, coaches must be resilient and persistent, with the ability to work under pressure and to handle criticism.

On the Job

Employers

In 2016, according to the Bureau of Labor Statistics (BLS), coaches in the United States were about evenly split between three employers: elementary and secondary schools; the arts, entertainment, and recreation industry; and colleges, universities, and professional schools. A smaller number of coaches were self-employed. Coaches may teach and train either professional or amateur athletes (including both adults and children). Possible job settings range from the NFL to high schools, where subject-area teachers and school administrators often work extra hours coaching school teams.

Working Conditions

Coaches who work with professional sports teams and athletes (and some who lead amateur teams and athletes) should expect to travel for competitions and events. If they coach an outdoor sport, they may work in extreme weather conditions, depending on the season. Hours may include evenings, weekends, and holidays, and extra hours may be required during competition season. For example, in an interview posted on the Bright Knowledge website, coach Stephen King explains that there is no such thing as a typical day at work:

> The worst part of my job is the long working days and the long working week: some days I leave for work at 7:30 a.m. and don't get back home until 8 p.m. Being a football coach is not a typical 9 to 5, Monday to Friday job. . . . Some days I may have a few hours off during the day and then have to coach until 10 p.m. as that is the only time players are available. I also work a seven-day week.

High school coaches often work part-time hours and also have a second job. Coaches in elementary, middle, and high schools may also coach multiple sports.

Earnings

According to the BLS, median pay for coaches (and scouts) in 2017 was $32,270, with salaries ranging from less than $18,670 (bottom 10 percent) to over $75,400 (upper 10 percent). College coaches usually earn more than high school coaches, and coaches who work for professional sports teams earn much more. In 2017 the highest-paid coaches working for the NBA, NFL, NHL, and MLB earned between $6 million and over $11 million annually. Alabama college football coach Nick Saban, reported on Business Insider in 2017 to be the highest-paid American college football coach, earned $11.15 million in 2017.

Opportunities for Advancement

Coaches may begin at the assistant coach entry level and advance to head coach, or they may move up from high school to college coaching. Pathways to coaching at the professional level include extensive coaching experience at lower levels, performance with a winning record in college sports, or success as a professional athlete. Many professional-level teams and athletes have head coaches, assistant coaches, and strength and conditioning coaches. The most prestigious and highest-paid coaching jobs are rarely advertised. Professional coaches who tend to advance to earn higher salaries or work for higher-rated teams usually have a record of winning games or of improving the performance of the teams they coach. Some coaches never advance beyond the level of their first coaching job. Many find professional fulfillment at the club, school, or recreational level.

What Is the Future Outlook for Coaches?

The future outlook for coaches is above average, with 13 percent growth expected through 2026. Increasing high school enrollment and a growing number of young athletes participating in high school and college sports are likely to create jobs. Applicants for high school coaching jobs who can also teach in a subject area or work as an administrator will be the strongest candidates. Coaches may also find newly available jobs as a result of the growing number of girls' and women's sports teams and the expanding sports programs and teams at smaller colleges.

Find Out More

Human Kinetics Coach Education Center
1607 N. Market St.
PO Box 5076
Champaign, IL 61825
website: www.asep.com

The Human Kinetics Coach Education Center offers the ASEP Professional Education Program, which includes courses and texts that lead to credentials for aspiring coaches at the high school, college, Olympic, and competitive club levels.

National Alliance for Youth Sports
2050 Vista Pkwy.
West Palm Beach, FL 33411
website: www.nays.org

The National Alliance for Youth Sports provides the most widely used coach training programs in the United States. The courses focus on two areas: coaching youth sports in general and sport-specific skills, fundamentals, and drills. The website also provides member services, including coaching resources and additional training materials.

National Association of State Boards of Education
333 John Carlyle St., Suite 530
Alexandria, VA 22314
website: www.nasbe.org

The National Association of State Boards of Education is a national nonprofit organization that represents the local boards of education that in turn oversee schools across America. Its website contains information about state-by-state requirements and standards for physical education in schools.

National High School Coaches Association
1 S. Third St., Suite 201
Easton, PA 18042
website: www.nhsca.com

The National High School Coaches Association supports high school coaches and their programs through educational programs, workshops, camps, publication of *Coaches Quarterly* magazine, coaching awards, and sponsorship of an Academic All-America team. The website provides resources and event information for athletes and coaches.

Sports Official

"Officiating is not for the faint of heart," advises the American Kinesiology Association in *Careers in Sports, Fitness, and Exercise*. This is because sports officials act as judges in a sports game, event, or competition, where emotions and tempers can be heated. There are different names for officials depending on the sport: baseball umpire, boxing referee, gymnastics judge, and so on. No matter what they are called, officials make sure that sporting events are fair and safe and that everyone follows the rules.

Before the event begins, officials in many sports check to make sure participants have proper and safe equipment and clothing. Barry Mano (founder of the National Association of Sports Officials and publisher of *Referee* magazine) affirms that keeping sports safe is a high priority for officials. Mano states in the Bureau of Labor Statistics' (BLS) *Occupational Outlook Quarterly*, "Our responsibility is to enforce impartially and err on the side of safety."

During events, sports officials communicate by using signals and

At a Glance

Sports Official

Minimum Educational Requirements
Varies; high school diploma or equivalent may be required

Personal Qualities
Communication skills, physical fitness, 20/20 eyesight, resilience, fairness

Certification and Licensing
Varies by employer and sport

Working Conditions
Indoors or outdoors, weather conditions vary, irregular hours, travel

Salary Range
About $18,360 to six-figure salaries annually (pay is usually per event)

Number of Jobs
About 21,100 in 2016

Future Job Outlook
Average job growth

tools appropriate to each sport (such as flags, whistles, and cards). They keep track of and enforce start and end times. When it is necessary to stop or pause an event, they are responsible for doing so. At the end of an event, it is often the official who declares the winner.

Officials must watch sporting events intently, positioning themselves in a spot where they can easily anticipate and observe the action and make sure all rules and standards of play are followed. Veteran NFL official and line judge Jeff Seeman reinforced this point in his public presentation at the 2017 Sports Officiating Summit (available on *Referee* magazine's website). He stated, "The secret to good judgment is seeing the action before it happens."

While they must be able to see the game clearly, officials also try not to interfere with the fans' line of vision. North Carolina basketball official Rob Livengood expresses this concern when he explains in the *Occupational Outlook Quarterly*, "I want to be invisible. The focus should be on the game, the players, and the fans." Unlike athletes and coaches, who can become famous when they are successful, many great sports officials remain more or less unnoticed as they go about their work of making the game or event run smoothly. Becoming a sports official is not likely to make anyone well-known to sports audiences—unless an official makes a serious mistake. In this case the official's ruling may be thoroughly discussed on television broadcasts and in the news media.

To ensure that all rules are followed and to minimize mistakes, depending on the sport, officials may work in groups or as individuals. For example, in professional baseball, four different umpires (one at home plate and one at every base) usually work together at a game. Football is another sport with multiple officials. Normally, there are seven officials in professional football, each with a specialty. Field judges, for example, determine whether passes crossed the goal line. In other sports, such as boxing, only one referee officiates.

When officials determine that a rule has been broken, or in response to an official complaint, they implement prescribed penalties. This responsibility makes the work of officials critical to the outcome of the game. It is also why the sports official job is not suited for those who fear unpopularity or conflict. Former British

Premier League, Football League, and FIFA referee Keith Hackett comments in the *Telegraph* that an official should expect to elicit hatred from at least half of the fans: "During those 90 minutes, what the referee is looking for is high levels of accuracy, decision making and integrity in terms of the performance. But you know you're going to upset half the spectators at one stage over the course of the match. That's the reality of the game."

Sports officials must use their best judgment to make high-stakes calls, knowing that their decisions may result in anger and outbursts from players, coaches, and spectators who disagree. Sometimes, individuals become so angry about official rulings that physical fights break out in the middle of a game. If a coach, spectator, or player becomes antagonistic or behaves in an otherwise inappropriate manner that interferes with the event, the sports official is authorized to eject that individual from the game.

Former sports official Barry Mano notes that officials develop "game intelligence" after many years of experience, which enables them to more easily manage events. With experience also comes the confidence needed to make and defend sometimes unpopular calls. However, sports officials sometimes make mistakes that may affect the outcome of a game or event. As sports author Fred Bowen writes in the *Washington Post*, "Everyone in sports—players, coaches and umpires—makes mistakes. Close calls, and even bad calls, are part of the game. Nobody's perfect." To minimize errors, officials in some sports use technology such as video replay to assist in making the correct call.

How Do You Become a Sports Official?

Education
States and sports athletic and activity associations have different educational and training requirements for sports officials. Some states require a high school diploma, and others do not. College is not officially required, but according to the US Department of Labor's CareerOneStop website, close to half of sports officials have a bachelor's degree. Some employers require sports officials

to complete specific training programs or seminars, both before and during employment.

In all cases, sports officials must demonstrate comprehensive knowledge of the rules of the sport in which they plan to work. Baseball umpires who work in the professional major and minor leagues attend specialized professional training schools, and college sports officials must attend officiating schools or programs. These programs cover topics including how to interpret sport-specific rules, good sportsmanship, and professional ethics. Training sessions and camps are also offered for those seeking jobs as officials in various sports.

Certification and Licensing

Certification and licensing requirements vary by employer. For jobs in which officials work with children, it is likely that certification will be required. Officials for high school sports must normally pass an officiating test on the rules of their sport and register with the appropriate state or local high school athletics agency. College sports officials are certified by officiating schools and must undergo a probationary period. Some associations require officials to renew their licenses yearly at training workshops. The National Association of Sports Officials is a starting point to learn about specific certification and licensing requirements.

Volunteer Work and Internships

A good way to get started and gain experience as a sports official is to contact local elementary schools or recreation centers to see if they provide volunteer opportunities. Sometimes youth soccer and hockey leagues employ beginning referees as part of a team that includes more experienced officials. Similarly, aspiring baseball umpires may find volunteer opportunities at their local Little League. School and club sports programs may also ask student athletes to work as officials when their team is not playing; this is another excellent opportunity to try out being a sports official.

Skills and Personality

Frequent arguments and complaints can make the job emotionally stressful, so a positive attitude is an important asset for sports officials. June Courteau is a basketball official and NCAA national coordinator of women's basketball officiating. In a public presentation at the 2017 Sports Officiating Summit (available on *Referee* magazine's website), Courteau advised, "Stay positive! Do you realize that 98 percent of what we do is good? It really is!" To withstand stressful responses after making unpopular calls, sports officials must be resilient, and they must value integrity and fairness over pleasing others. Since sports officials must make quick and fair judgments and relay these to athletes, coaches, and spectators, excellent communication and decision-making skills are important assets.

Physically, depending on the sport, officials must be in good condition and capable of running, jogging, sprinting, squatting, or standing for long periods. For example, football and soccer referees must run in order to remain in an advantageous viewing position on the field. Hockey referees must skate. Linesmen stand for long periods. This is a job for people with 20/20 eyesight and excellent observation and concentration abilities.

On the Job

Employers

Employers for sports officials include K–12 schools, community youth recreation leagues, sports clubs, corporate leagues, college athletics departments, and professional and semiprofessional sports organizations.

Working Conditions

Many sports officials have another main job. They may work in sports to supplement their income or because they want to stay involved with a sport they love. Typically, the hours are irregular, including weekends, evenings, and holidays. Depending on the sport, officials may work either indoors or outdoors. Work sites may include neighborhood parks, school or YMCA gyms, college athletic centers, or professional sports stadiums. Weather conditions can be challenging. When football is played on a snowy field, for example, the referees must be out in the snow along with the

Umpires-in-training learn how to track a baseball without moving their heads, part of a course that teaches the fundamentals and fine points of umpiring. Sports officials who work in professional leagues are often required to attend such courses.

athletes. Travel is typically local at the lower levels, but college- and professional-level officials should expect cross-country or even international travel.

Earnings

Entry-level salaries are low for sports officials. The median pay for referees, umpires, and sports officials in 2017 was $26,800, according to the BLS. Annual earnings in the lowest 10 percent of the range were less than $18,360, while the highest 10 percent exceeded $56,100. Officials are normally paid per game. As may be expected, professional sports officials earn significantly more than high school and college sports officials. The highest-paid professional officials earn hundreds of thousands of dollars per year.

Opportunities for Advancement

Beginning sports officials tend to work in either youth sports or high school freshman sports. From there, advancement opportunities may lead to junior varsity, varsity, college, and professional sports. Typically, many years of experience at each level and extremely solid performance and knowledge of rules are required to advance. High-level positions are very competitive. For example, professional-level baseball umpires normally work in the minor leagues for at least seven years before they may be considered for a position in the major leagues.

What Is the Future Outlook for Sports Officials?

According to the BLS, jobs for referees, umpires, and other sports officials are expected to see average growth of 8 percent through 2026. This estimate parallels predicted general population growth and the resulting projected increases in future high school enrollment and participation in organized sports. Also, sports at small colleges and women's sports are predicted to expand, which should create additional jobs. Since college and professional jobs are extremely competitive and normally go to highly experienced candidates, those entering the profession for the first time are more likely to find jobs at the high school or recreational levels.

Find Out More

International Association of Approved Basketball Officials (IAABO)
PO Box 355
Carlisle, PA 17013
website: https://iaabo.org

The IAABO is a nonprofit service and professional organization for basketball referees. The website provides details about its summer officiating schools, meetings, seminars, *Sportorials* newsletter, governance, and more.

Minor League Baseball
9550 Sixteenth St. N.
St. Petersburg, FL 33716
website: www.milb.com

The Umpires section of the Minor League Baseball website contains helpful information about how to become a baseball umpire. Included is information about Minor League Baseball Umpire Development, umpire camps and schools, salaries, and umpire manuals.

National Association of Sports Officials (NASO)
2017 Lathrop Ave.
Racine, WI 53405
website: www.naso.org

The NASO is a nonprofit membership organization that provides information, programs, and services to sports officials. Its website includes extensive information, including a Becoming an Official section, insurance, links to special reports and relevant legislation, publications, and more.

National Federation of State High School Associations (NFHS)
PO Box 690
Indianapolis, IN 46206
website: www.nfhs.org

The NFHS establishes and disseminates the rules for sixteen sports played in US high schools. Its website contains detailed information about the rules of the sports it oversees, as well as sport-specific resources for officials who wish to work in high schools.

Referee
2017 Lathrop Ave.
Racine, WI 53405
website: www.referee.com

Referee is an industry-specific subscription-based magazine. Its website offers resources of interest to sports officials, including discussions of job-related issues by leading sports officials, sports rosters and quizzes, merchandise, links to college conferences and contact information, and free informational guides.

Athletic Trainer

What Does an Athletic Trainer Do?

In a high school lacrosse game, Tommy Mallon collided with another player and fell to the ground. Mallon's impulse was to get back into the game after what seemed like a normal fall. Fortunately, on-site athletic trainer Riki Kirchhoff assessed the situation and did not allow him to get up. It turned out that Mallon's neck was broken, and blood was leaking from an artery. Had he tried to stand up after what appeared to be a normal sport injury, he would have died. Mallon survived and, with his mother, Beth Mallon, subsequently founded the nonprofit organization Advocates for Injured Athletes. The organization employs athletic trainers to educate sports teams about the signs and symptoms of sports-related injuries and to advocate for the presence of a certified athletic trainer in every high school in the United States.

When athletes like Tommy Mallon become injured or ill, athletic trainers are usually the first health care providers to diagnose and treat them at the scene. Therefore, athletic trainers must be present at games and training sessions. Since many trainers are former athletes or sports fans, this is an enjoyable

At a Glance

Athletic Trainer

Minimum Educational Requirements
Bachelor's degree

Personal Qualities
Patience, communication skills, compassion, decisiveness

Certification and Licensing
Required in most states

Working Conditions
Indoors or outdoors, weather conditions vary, irregular hours, travel

Salary Range
About $30,740 to $69,530 or more

Number of Jobs
About 27,800 in 2016

Future Job Outlook
Better than average

part of the job for most. However, when trainers watch a game, they cannot focus too much on the score or the outcome of the game. Instead, they try to see injuries when they happen in order to know how best to respond. Retired Utah Jazz athletic trainer Gary Briggs explains why this part of his job is important in an article on the NBA website: "If I see what (injury) actually occurred, it may help me to know the seriousness of it. If the player says, 'oh, my knee hurts,' I can say, 'I saw you got hit from the outside, or you hyperextended it.' I need to watch the floor to see how they got hurt."

Depending on the injury, treatment may include first aid procedures such as reducing swelling with ice, keeping cuts clean to prevent infection, bracing or bandaging injured body parts, or providing crutches until a doctor or emergency medical technician may be seen. In serious cases such as a fracture, athletic trainers arrange for immediate medical care in an emergency room. Any serious injuries must be diagnosed and treated by a physician, and only physicians may prescribe medication. However, athletic trainers may treat minor injuries under the direction of a physician and other health care providers.

When the injury has improved, athletic trainers help oversee rehabilitation and evaluate readiness to reenter the sport, as directed by a physician. Trainers help athletes design and implement a physical program to regain flexibility, strength, speed, range of motion, and balance. High school athletic trainer Amy Virden notes that supervising each athlete's recovery plan requires adaptability and vigilance. In an interview published in the *Inquirer*, she reflects, "No two athletes are alike and no two injuries are alike. The way one athlete responds and recovers from an ankle sprain can be totally different from the way another athlete responds and recovers." Sometimes athletes try to return to their sport before they are physically ready. It is the trainer's job to prevent reinjury by deciding when an injured athlete has actually healed sufficiently.

In addition to responding to injuries, athletic trainers work to prevent injuries before they happen. For example, trainers educate athletes and coaches about the use of protective gear and devices. They also develop personalized exercise and nutrition programs. Trainers also examine athletes and identify preexisting medical conditions that require precautions, and they work with coaches to modify practice regimens that might lead to overuse injuries. Charlie Thompson, head of athletic training at a New Jersey university, explains in the Bureau of Labor Statistics' (BLS) *Occupational Outlook Quarterly* how trainers use their knowledge of sport-specific injuries to help coaches keep their athletes injury-free. According to Thompson, "We can prevent injuries by removing or minimizing specific drills or exercises on days the athletes need a break." Athletic trainers also make sure that sports programs comply with legal safety regulations around potential injuries such as concussions.

Another part of the daily responsibilities of athletic trainers is administrative work. Trainers must be sure that medical supplies and safety equipment are on hand. Athletic trainers must also keep records, write reports, and attend meetings regarding issues such as expenditures on safety equipment or implementation of injury-prevention policies.

How Do You Become an Athletic Trainer?

Education

Amy Virden, in an interview with the *Inquirer* (Philadelphia), advises aspiring trainers to be prepared for challenging educational requirements. Says Virden:

> If you like sports and have always wanted to work in service to others, do it. That being said, it is not an easy path to become an athletic trainer. Many colleges have selective admission into their athletic training educational programs. The coursework is challenging and fairly science heavy. Each student must demonstrate proficiency in a variety of practical applications on the field, then pass a national certification exam to work as an athletic trainer. It might sound demanding but it is worth it.

High school students who are interested in this career path may begin by taking anatomy, physiology, and physics courses. As Virden suggests, most employers require a minimum of a bachelor's degree from an accredited athletic training program, which will likely include courses in biology, anatomy, physiology, nutrition, and other related subjects. Securing a job with a college or at the professional level generally requires a master's degree in athletic training or a field such as sport psychology, along with prior experience as a trainer. According to the National Athletic Trainers' Association, over 70 percent of athletic trainers have completed a master's degree.

Certification and Licensing

Most states require successful completion of an educational program accredited by the Commission on Accreditation of Athletic Training Education, followed by a national certification exam overseen by the Board of Certification for the Athletic Trainer. Trainers should expect to renew their cardiopulmonary resuscitation certification every year and to participate in ongoing classes, seminars, and lectures to stay current in their knowledge of the field. According to the *Occupational Outlook Quarterly*, trainers must complete seventy hours of ongoing education every three years. They must also continue to comply with the Board of Certification's Standards of Professional Practice.

Volunteer Work and Internships

Some high schools, colleges, and hospitals provide volunteer opportunities under the supervision of athletic trainers. The University of Georgia offers a three-day annual workshop for high school students who are considering a career as an athletic trainer. Coveted and competitive student internships with professional teams are also offered by organizations such as the Professional Baseball Athletic Trainers Society and the Professional Football Athletic Trainers Society. Some accredited athletic training educational programs offer internships for students as a way to gain preprofessional experience. Chris Olson, for example, completed an internship with a baseball team in the Dominican Republic while he was a master's degree student at Florida International University's Athletic Training Program. Olson explains in an article on the university's website how the internship boosted his professional confidence.

He remembers, "My greatest concern in the beginning was my confidence in my ability to be able to say about an injury, 'this is what it is.' But by the end of the internship, I was able to do that and come up with new ideas about treatments and rehab exercises. My confidence skyrocketed out of the roof."

Skills and Personality

Patience and good listening and communication skills are important personality traits. High school athletic trainer Tricia Irvin, who works for a medical center in Granger, Indiana, says in the *Occupational Outlook Quarterly*, "We listen to their [athletes'] problems and try to guide them in the right direction. You need to be patient." Compassion is an important personality trait for dealing with athletes in pain. Excellent decision-making skills and a level head are critical, since trainers are the first on the scene and must sometimes diagnose potentially life-threatening or life-altering injuries.

On the Job

Employers

According to the BLS, most trainers work at colleges and universities, hospitals, sports medicine clinics, and medical offices. Athletic trainers who work in orthopedic doctors' offices are sometimes called physician extenders. Military bases also hire athletic trainers to help rehabilitate injured personnel, and athletic trainers also work with Olympic athletes. Some athletic trainers are employed in the performing arts industry, helping dancers, musicians, and vocalists prevent and seek treatment for occupational injuries.

Many, but not all, high schools employ athletic trainers. Because of budget constraints, some trainers work for more than one team and are paid hourly or on contract. Philadelphia athletic trainer Amy Virden, for example, who was profiled in the *Inquirer*, works with one other athletic trainer at her school to cover fifty-two middle school and high school teams. She travels from one field to the next on a golf cart.

An athletic trainer checks a player's twisted ankle. Assessing the severity of an injury is one job of the athletic trainer. They also provide immediate care, such as bandaging cuts, icing sprains, stabilizing breaks, and evaluating players for concussions.

Working Conditions

Depending on the sport, trainers may work indoors or outdoors, sometimes in extreme weather conditions. Most athletic trainers work full time, and those who work for teams may travel and work evenings and weekends. They spend many working hours in gyms, locker rooms, and athletic fields. Their work brings them regularly into high-pressure and emotionally stressful situations, in which they must make quick, informed decisions and deal with athletes in pain.

Earnings

According to the BLS, median pay for athletic trainers in 2017 was $46,630 per year. Earnings per year ranged from less than $30,740 (lowest 10 percent) to over $69,530 (highest 10 percent). Author Shelly Field states in *Career Opportunities in the Sports Industry* that athletic trainers working for professional teams may earn much higher salaries, depending on the type and level of the team and the trainers' responsibilities.

Opportunities for Advancement

There is a clear path to advancement in this field. Trainers begin at the entry level as assistant athletic trainers and progress to higher levels as head athletic trainers. They may also become athletic directors, or they may go on to work in management as administrators in hospitals or clinics. For those who begin their career with a bachelor's degree, acquiring a master's or other advanced degree is important to attaining job mobility.

What Is the Future Outlook for Athletic Trainers?

With recent increasing public interest in protecting athletes from potentially life-altering injuries, the athletic trainer profession appears to have a bright future. The BLS predicts rapid job growth of 23 percent through 2026. A major factor inspiring this growth is knowledge of the effect of concussions on the developing brains of children who play sports. While not every school has a budget for an athletic trainer, some US states require athletic trainers in public secondary school sports programs. Also, because more middle-aged and older adults continue to play sports, athletic trainers are needed to prevent and treat injuries among this population.

Find Out More

Board of Certification for the Athletic Trainer
1415 Harney St., Suite 200
Omaha, NE 68102
website: www.bocatc.org

The Board of Certification for the Athletic Trainer establishes and oversees the certification program for US athletic trainers. Its website contains standards of professional practice for the profession as well as a list of providers and detailed information about how to become certified.

College Athletic Trainers' Society

Dinsmore & Shohl, LLP
1 Oxford Centre
301 Grant St., Suite 2800
Pittsburgh, PA 15219
website: www.collegeathletictrainer.org

The College Athletic Trainers' Society was founded by athletic trainers to address the specific needs and concerns of athletic trainers working at colleges and universities. The website includes a career center with job postings, information about symposia and scholarships, and recent news pertaining to the field.

Commission on Accreditation of Athletic Training Education (CAATE)

6850 Austin Center Blvd., Suite 100
Austin, TX 78731
website: https://caate.net

The CAATE is the only organization that oversees accreditation of hundreds of educational programs for athletic trainers. Its website includes a search tool for accredited educational programs and an FAQ section for students who wish to become athletic trainers.

National Athletic Trainers' Association (NATA)

1620 Valwood Pkwy., Suite 115
Carrollton, TX 75006
website: www.nata.org

The NATA is a professional membership organization for certified trainers and those who support the profession. The organization's website offers a wide range of resources, including resources for trainers in different types of job settings and a section with job listings, professional development, and educational events.

Sports Announcer

In 2016 Anheuser-Busch released a widely viewed video that addressed the public role of sports announcers as the voice of their team. That year, the Chicago Cubs baseball team finally ended its legendary seventy-one-year "curse" and won the World Series. By combining recordings from previous broadcasts with video from the winning game, the Anheuser-Busch video made it appear as if the iconic Cubs announcer Harry Caray, who had died in 1998, was calling the Cubs' victory in the last play of the game. The video provoked an emotional response from many Cubs fans who still identified Caray as the voice of the team because of his years as a Cubs announcer.

Sports announcers like Caray interpret and comment on what is happening during an athletic game, competition, or event for a live and/or broadcast audience. This is especially helpful for radio audiences, who cannot see the game. In addition to play-by-play reporting, sports announcers typically list the players in the starting lineup, announce players as they come into a game or competition,

At a Glance

Sports Announcer

Minimum Educational Requirements
Varies

Personal Qualities
Interpersonal skills, clear speaking voice, dependability, quick thinking, good memory

Certification and Licensing
Optional

Working Conditions
Indoors or outdoors, weather conditions vary, irregular hours, travel

Salary Range
About $18,000 to $83,000; some celebrity announcers earn in the millions

Number of Jobs
About 52,700 in 2016

Future Job Outlook
Limited

and read public service announcements and advertisements from sponsors. Sometimes they interview athletes, coaches, managers, or fans, and may moderate discussions. On many radio, television, and Internet broadcasts, play-by-play announcers narrate the events of the game while color commentators (usually former players or coaches) add additional information based on their expert knowledge. Announcers who work for radio or television may also operate studio equipment or perform supportive technical broadcasting tasks. Many announcers maintain an Internet or print media presence, including social networking and writing for blogs or sports publications.

An important part of an announcer's job is advance research. Sports announcers must know the rules, statistics, and history of the sport. They should also be aware of related developments in sports news and detailed information about the teams, coaches, and players. NBC announcer Mike Tirico shares his personal research routine in a story published on the NFL News website. During the week before an upcoming game, Tirico watches prior games of the teams he will announce, studies related videos, calls contacts in the league, and visits both teams' practices and meetings. Longtime hockey announcer Doug McLeod adds that it is important to develop a method to quickly access research during a broadcast. He explains in an interview posted on the Work in Sports website, "We all have our individual ways of coming in organized. Some work better than others. The important thing is to experiment with different spotting charts and ways of organizing notes, whether on paper or something compact like a tablet."

The day of a sporting event typically begins for an announcer with final research, production meetings, pregame and preproduction tasks, setup and review of notes, practicing text that must be read, and meeting with other media and team representatives. At the event, announcers interpret the details of the game to promote better understanding and engagement than audiences could achieve on their own. They tell stories, insert important details and context, and explain the importance of plays. In an interview posted on the career blog *Work in Sports*, sports broadcaster John Strong stresses the importance of good storytelling skills: "Storytelling is just as relevant in play-by-play as when I was doing sports updates on the radio. Things like having a great voice are sometimes overrated. This business is all about telling stories." Many announcers record their sessions and later review their performance to identify mistakes and areas for improvement.

How Do You Become a Sports Announcer?

Education

When asked by the NFL News website what advice he would give someone entering the field, Mike Tirico noted that there is no set path. He suggested that hopeful announcers find ways to practice with the goal of developing a style that may appeal to a future employer. He pointed out, "This is a job that there is no bar exam for. You're hired very often by the enjoyment of your style from the one person who's doing the hiring, so you can't think, 'Do this, this and this and you'll get the job.'"

As Tirico suggests, educational requirements to become a sports announcer vary. Most announcers have at least a high school diploma, but this may not be required for some public address announcer positions. For radio and television announcers, an undergraduate degree in a field such as journalism, communications, or sports broadcasting may be necessary. Courses that develop strong writing and speaking skills are advisable. It is a good idea to select a college that has an on-campus radio and/or television station or one that is located near a local station that allows undergraduates to acquire announcing experience. Detailed familiarity with the sport to be announced is required. Experience playing or writing about sports is also helpful. New announcers may receive on-the-job training to familiarize them with audio and production equipment.

Certification and Licensing

Typically, certificates or licenses are not required by employers. However, the National Association of Sports Public Address Announcers (NASPAA) offers an online certification course for public address announcers. Topics include the announcer's code of conduct, pregame/event responsibilities, safety and security issues, and announcing "do's and don'ts." Each year, the NAS-PAA also offers public address–announcing clinics around the country.

Volunteer Work and Internships

Live announcing requires practice, so volunteer work and internships are highly recommended. Most employers expect applicants to have some experience. Announcers who work as volunteers and interns can develop a portfolio of recordings of their best performances for job applications.

Some high schools and recreational leagues offer volunteer opportunities. College students may volunteer as announcers for college sports events at college radio or television stations. Internships may be available at local radio stations.

The Internet is an especially promising source of volunteer opportunities, and enterprising candidates may be able to find volunteer announcing positions by contacting streaming stations that cover sports. This is how John Strong made his start when he was a junior in high school. In an interview that appears on the *Work in Sports* blog, he remembers how he found his first job:

The OSAA (Oregon State Athletic Association) had done webcasts of the previous year's football semis and final, so I e-mailed to ask if I could be a part in any way. They pointed me to a new website that had just launched, basically a one-step webcasting service, which was looking for exactly what we were: parents or kids that wanted to do High School football. . . .

Understand this was 2002, when no one was podcasting or doing webcasting other than a few radio stations just putting their signal on the internet; we were one of maybe ten student programs that fall. It was incredibly rough, incredibly low tech, but it was play-by-play.

With the explosion of Internet-based media since 2002, today's aspiring announcers may do well to follow Strong's lead by looking for unadvertised online announcing opportunities.

For those who cannot find volunteer opportunities or internships (or who need experience before applying for these opportunities), Doug McLeod emphasizes the value of practicing at home. In his tips for job seekers on the *Work in Sports* blog, McLeod recommends calling games while watching television or a computer screen. This technique proved valuable for Beth Mowins, who made history in 2017 as the first woman play-by-play announcer to call an NFL game for CBS. Mowins states in an interview on the CBS News website, "I've always looked at myself as a play-by-play announcer. I've been calling the NFL since I was about 8 years old, in my living room, so it's not new to me, it's just new to everybody else." Mowins notes the "10,000-hour rule," which is shorthand for the hours of hard work hopeful announcers must dedicate to practicing their skills.

Skills and Personality

To excel as a sports announcer, it is necessary to have excellent public speaking and research skills. Interpersonal skills are also important. Announcers often interview players immediately after a major win or loss, when emotions run high, and they must be able to formulate appropriate questions. Announcers who plan to work on television should take an interest in personal style and appearance, and all announcers should have a clear speaking voice and excellent command of grammar, pronunciation, and timing.

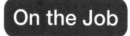

On the Job

Employers

Sports announcers are employed in industries that include spectator sports and entertainment, television and radio broadcast, and public address system announcing. Public address announcers provide live commentary over a system that uses microphones, amplifiers, and loudspeakers to make them audible to the crowd.

Announcers who work in radio and television are called broadcasters or newscasters. In this case, play-by-play announcing may be only one part of their job. They may also provide pre- and postgame coverage, host television or radio talk shows or podcasts, or report on sports throughout the day.

Working Conditions

Many sports announcers work in comfortable indoor recording studios or booths at athletic fields or gymnasiums. Some announcers travel with a particular team to announce at "away" sporting events. Most work full time, but there are also part-time opportunities for sports announcers. Irregular and often long or unusual hours may include weekends, evenings, and holidays.

Earnings

There is a wide range in annual pay for sports announcers. Entry-level jobs tend to offer very low pay. On the other end of the spectrum, celebrity announcer and sportscaster Bob Costas is reported to take home an annual salary of $7 million, according to Bankrate. Salaries in the millions, however, are not the norm. The Bureau of Labor Statistics (BLS) reports that 2017 median pay for announcers, including sports announcers, was $31,500 annually. As a whole, radio and television announcers (a category that includes sports announcers) earned annual pay from less than $18,840 to over $83,520. Similarly, for public address and other announcers (including sports announcers), annual earnings ranged from less than $18,330 to more than $81,410. Announcers working in larger markets tend to earn higher pay than announcers in smaller markets.

Opportunities for Advancement

Landing a first job as a sports announcer is very competitive. Some beginning sports announcers start by working for college radio stations, Minor League Baseball teams, small college football teams, and Internet broadcasters. Job seekers are most likely to find work at radio or television stations in small towns with small media markets. Advancement normally happens when a sports announcer moves to a higher-level job at a larger market station in a bigger city.

What Is the Future Outlook for Sports Announcers?

Sports announcing is not a high-growth career. The BLS predicts declining job opportunities for radio and television announcers, but through 2026, a slight increase for public address system and other announcers. One area of possible future job growth, according to the BLS, is the emergence of Internet radio stations and podcasts. Another hopeful development is the possibility of new announcer jobs as a result of the incorporation of local coverage into national and satellite news programs.

Find Out More

Broadcast Education Association
1771 N St. NW
Washington, DC 20036
website: www.beaweb.org/wp

This international organization focuses on preparing college students for television and radio careers, as well as providing academic support to professionals and educators in the industry. The organization provides resources related to teaching and research, publishes several industry journals, and holds an annual conference.

National Association of Broadcasters
1771 N St. NW
Washington, DC 20036
website: www.nab.org

The National Association of Broadcasters is a trade association and advocacy group for US radio and television broadcasters.

Its website contains many advocacy and education resources for members and nonmembers, as well as links to resources and services for those working in the broadcasting profession.

National Association of Digital Broadcasters
website: http://thenadb.org

Self-described as "advocates for radio's new generation," this organization provides advocacy and programming assistance for webcasters and other streaming stations. It provides resources such as development guidelines and jingle producers for its members.

National Association of Sports Public Address Announcers (NASPAA)
website: https://www.naspaa.net

The NASPAA is a professional organization that represents both sports public address announcers and their employers. The group offers professional development (including online courses and clinics), a job board, membership benefits, and other services.

NCTA—The Internet & Television Association
25 Massachusetts Ave. NW, Suite 100
Washington, DC 20001
website: www.ncta.com

Formerly known as the National Cable Television Association, this organization is the main trade association for the US cable television and broadband industries. The group engages in advocacy activities around issues such as net neutrality, and it publishes industry-related data and news on its website.

Sportswriter

What Does a Sportswriter Do?

After working at the *Washington Post* for over thirty years (including twenty years as a sports columnist), Michael Wilbon wrote in his farewell column in 2010 that he was leaving "the best job in America." He deeply appreciated the opportunities he had as a sportswriter to cover and shape public understanding of sporting events. He noted that, when he first began his job at the newspaper,

> it never dawned on me I'd wind up covering nine Olympic Games for *The Post*, or more than 20 Super Bowls, more than 20 Final Fours, more than 20 NBA Finals, or more importantly evolve to the point where the editors of this newspaper would trust me to lead the daily discussion about the news of the day and the changing cultural landscape as it all related to sports.

Sportswriters like Wilbon are journalists who specialize in writing

At a Glance

Sportswriter

Minimum Educational Requirements
Bachelor's and/or master's degree in journalism or communication is advised

Personal Qualities
Resourceful, dependable, good communicator, persistent

Working Conditions
Irregular hours, frequent travel, strict deadlines, excellent seats at sporting events

Salary Range
About $22,970 to $2 million or more

Number of Jobs
About 50,400 in 2016 (all reporters, correspondents, and broadcast news analysts, a category that includes sportswriters)

Future Job Outlook
Limited

about sports news for media publications. They typically work for newspapers, magazines, sports websites, team websites, blogs, and other digital and print publications. Sportswriters conduct research and produce articles with content such as scores reports; in-depth event and game analysis; feature stories; profiles of athletes, teams, and managers; and coverage of industry trends and policies. Top sportswriters with loyal readerships author regular columns that express their editorial views, opinions, or analysis of sports topics and events. Some sportswriters contribute to television or radio broadcasts.

Wherever they work, sportswriters have a busy and hectic schedule. They often attend games in the evenings and spend their daytime hours writing stories, interviewing sources, pitching new story ideas to editors, and conducting research. To meet deadlines for reports on sporting events, they may start writing before the game has even finished.

The types of articles assigned to a sportswriter depend on the publication. Sportswriters who work for newspapers or websites are sometimes assigned to a beat, meaning that they always cover a particular sport, team, or sports topic. Magazine-based sportswriters tend to write longer and more in-depth stories with a broader focus. *Sports Illustrated* writer Peter King, in a profile published on the website Bleacher Report, observes that media companies with websites tend to offer expanded opportunities to their journalists. He says, "We've gotten into an era in journalism where if you work for a company that has a prominent website, you are not only asked to be a reporter for that website, you are also asked to be a columnist and an opinion setter."

Whatever their assignment, sportswriters are expected to continually study events and individuals in their field and to keep track of scores, statistics, and sports-related news and human-interest stories. Sportswriters conduct research by attending sporting events and press conferences and interviewing players, managers, coaches, and other sports representatives. When they report on out-of-town sporting events, they rely on national and international wire services for scores, statistics, and other vital information. Also, sportswriters consult the reports of stringers, or sports journalists who cover lower-profile events.

In addition to reporting the scores and other details of sporting events, sportswriters provide in-depth coverage of broader issues for readers. For example, after a local team loses an important competition, a sportswriter may analyze the possible reasons for the loss and how the team's performance relates to its history. In feature stories, sportswriters may cover industry trends such as new safety regulations, the use of technology by sports officials, or gender issues in sports. Beat reporters may write about coaches' and players' lives on and off the field.

These types of stories often require close working relationships with team members, coaches, and staff. For example, *ESPN The Magazine* senior writer Mina Kimes's first cover story was about New York Jets football player Darrelle Revis. Kimes chose to focus on Revis's negotiating skills and career management. In an interview on the website ESPN Front Row, Kimes explains that her greatest challenge was making Revis feel comfortable discussing his career with her:

> The most difficult part of reporting this story was getting Revis to open up—he's extremely gracious, but also extremely reserved, and he isn't prone to telling long anecdotes or dishing out opinions, especially when it comes to off-the-field stuff. With a profile subject like that, getting a great deal of access is key. We spent a couple of days together, so the conversation was pretty organic.

Kimes's story about Revis is an example of sportswriting in which the author develops a unique angle to bring new knowledge about sports figures to readers. To engage readers and address original topics, sportswriters assess what is being covered already—and how—by reading the work of their peers. Then they develop their own unique style and perspectives. For example, *Slate* reporter Josh Levin describes ESPN senior writer Zach Lowe as the "sports writer smart fans deserve." Levin notes that Lowe draws from a variety of multimedia sources to educate and entertain his readers and analyze big questions and events in sports. Levin explains:

> His columns are basketball tutorials, articles that draw on stats, video cut-ups, and interviews with players and coaches to teach you how the sport works. Lowe's prose is clear, but it isn't dry; his writing crackles with a kind of conspiratorial glee, like he can't wait to share all the cool stuff he's just figured out. Lowe's pieces and podcasts help the rest of us become better basketball consumers, and they make watching the NBA more fun.

Lowe's use of videos and images in his online stories is an example of the multimedia sports journalism increasingly used by online publications as well as print publications with online editions. In multimedia sports journalism, sportswriters gather and use videos, photographs, and audio recording to enhance coverage. Many sportswriters also connect with their audience through active use of social media. For example, ESPN football reporter Adam Schefter uses Twitter to comment on breaking news; he had over 7 million followers in 2018.

How Do You Become a Sportswriter?

Education

It is generally necessary for a sportswriter to have a bachelor's degree in journalism, communications, or English. Many sportswriters have master's degrees in these fields.

Certification and Licensing

Certification and licensing are not typically required by employers. Some schools, such as the Frank W. and Sue Mayborn School of Journalism at the University of North Texas and the University of North Carolina School of Media and Journalism, offer a certificate program in sports journalism or sports communication.

Volunteer Work and Internships

Mike Lupica, a sportswriter for over forty years, says his first important education in the profession was as a volunteer. He recalls in the *Washington Post*, "My journalism school was that I wrote for three school newspapers when I was at Boston College. I also wrote articles for the *Boston Globe and Boston Phoenix*."

Decades later, the importance of volunteer experience and a strong portfolio for aspiring sportswriters remains strong. Fortunately, many volunteer opportunities are available for aspiring sportswriters. High school and college students may cover school sports for their school or community newspapers and yearbooks. College journalism programs typically include internships with community employers, college sports information departments, or under the supervision of established beat reporters at sports websites or newspapers.

Skills and Personality

A flair for writing and an excellent command of grammar are important skills for a sportswriter. Organization, research skills, resourcefulness, dependability, and the ability to meet deadlines are critical. While it is helpful to have played a sport, player experience is not a requirement for sportswriters—a thorough and up-to-date knowledge of sports is usually sufficient. Sportswriters must know the rules of the sport they cover as well as athletes and coaches do. Also, an outgoing personality, interpersonal communication skills, and persistence are all necessary for conducting interviews.

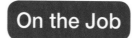

On the Job

Employers

Employment options for sportswriters are varied. Possibilities include print newspapers and magazines, news websites, team and sporting league websites, blogs, and sometimes radio and television. Many news publications contain sports sections, and some (such as *Sports Illustrated*, *Sports Business Daily*, and

ESPN The Magazine) are solely dedicated to sports coverage. Some sportswriters are self-employed as freelance writers for a variety of publications. Freelance writers are usually paid per published article, and they must look for work between assignments.

Working Conditions

According to ESPN New York editor Matt Marrone, it is important that sportswriters love their job, because the working conditions are challenging. When asked by *Forbes* contributor Catey Hill to provide advice for aspiring sportswriters, Marrone cautioned, "If you want a set schedule, with nights and weekends off—or if you want to be rich—find another line of work! That being said, I am proud to tell people what I do for a living; I know I'll never cure cancer, but at least I can share my love of writing and my passion for news to serve sports fans."

As Marrone's advice suggests, aspiring sportswriters should expect to work irregular hours, including weekends, evenings, and holidays, and to travel frequently. Strict deadlines may require sportswriters to work long hours, including late at night. An urgent breaking story necessitates work during unscheduled times. Sportswriters whose beat is to cover a specific team may go on the road with the team, which can mean being away from home much of the year. Sportswriters attend frequent sporting events (where they are provided with excellent press seats and opportunities to interview sports celebrities) and press conferences. Some sports reporters have no office and work from home or on-the-go with a laptop.

Earnings

According to the Bureau of Labor Statistics (BLS), the 2017 median annual pay for reporters and correspondents (a category that includes sportswriters) was $39,370, and annual pay ranged from less than $22,970 (lowest 10 percent) to over $90,540 (highest 10 percent). Sportswriters for major magazines, writers with syndicated columns, and those who work in radio or television are likely to earn higher-than-average salaries.

Opportunities for Advancement

Competition for sportswriting jobs is high, but there are opportunities for advancement for writers who are willing to relocate. Moving from a smaller market to a larger market is a typical path. For many starting writers, this means taking a first job at a small newspaper in a small town to gain the experience needed to advance to a major publication in a city. Some beginning sportswriters may also find starter jobs with sports websites, where it is easier to find work than in print media. Another option is to begin as a stringer and move up to a higher-paid position and more high-profile assignments. After building up an online portfolio, experienced website writers may move on to positions with print publications. Sportswriters already working in print media move up to positions as editors or full-time columnists.

What Is the Future Outlook for Sportswriters?

Sportswriting is not a high-growth career. The BLS predicts declining job opportunities for reporters, correspondents, and broadcast news analysts (a grouping that includes sportswriters) through 2026. Jobs at Internet publications offer the best outlook for sportswriters, with more opportunities online for writing and blogging about sports, especially in multimedia journalism.

Find Out More

Associated Press Sports Editors
PO Box 699
Huntington, NY 11743
website: http://apsportseditors.com

This organization seeks to improve the professional standards of its extensive network of member media organizations. The group administers a job board, diversity fellowships, an annual conference, writing awards, and student sports journalism contests.

Association for Women in Sports Media

21317 Estero Preserve Run
Estero, FL 33928
website: http://awsmonline.org

This organization of male and female members is dedicated to providing support and advocacy for women sports media professionals. The group offers networking and mentoring initiatives, an internship/scholarship program, regional events, an annual summer conference, and the Mary Garber Pioneer Award to honor individuals who have paved the way for women in sports media.

Baseball Writers' Association of America

website: https://bbwaa.com

This organization, founded in 1908, supports sports journalists who work for publications that cover Major League Baseball. Its active members elect players to the National Baseball Hall of Fame and vote for annual baseball awards, including Most Valuable Player, Cy Young, Rookie of the Year, and Manager of the Year.

National Sports Media Association

PO Box 5394
Winston-Salem, NC 27113
website: https://nationalsportsmedia.org

Formerly known as the National Sportscasters and Sportswriters Association, this is a membership group for sports media professionals and students. The group develops educational opportunities, including internships, scholarships, mentorships, and networking, and it honors sports media professionals with a Hall of Fame and several awards.

Pro Football Writers of America

website: www.profootballwriters.org

This organization advocates for sports journalists who cover professional football by working to gain access to NFL personnel. The organization confers the Dick Connor Writing Award and numerous on-field and off-field awards for individuals and teams in professional football.

Sport Psychologist

What Does a Sport Psychologist Do?

In the tense moments before she begins each rotation in competitions, gymnast and US Olympic medalist Laurie Hernandez places her right hand on her stomach, closes her eyes, and takes a deep breath. This is a relaxation technique she learned from her sport psychologist, Robert Andrews. Andrews also helped another high-profile client, gymnast Simone Biles, overcome her anxiety and prepare for the World Championship after her disappointing performance at a prior competition in 2013. Biles went on to become a gold medalist at the 2016 Summer Olympics. She reflects in an interview posted on the Full Twist gymnastics website, "Finding ways to calm down was really important. I found that I was getting too intense. Working with Robert also helped ease my fears and I found more confidence."

Sport psychologists study and apply psychological factors that affect sports behavior and performance. According to the American Psychological Association (APA), sport psychologists work in areas

At a Glance

Sport Psychologist

Minimum Educational Requirements
Doctoral degree in psychology

Personal Qualities
Compassionate, excellent communication and interpersonal skills, highly ethical

Certification and Licensing
Psychologists in clinical practice must be licensed; most states require certification

Working Conditions
Hours and work settings may vary, part-time or full-time, possible travel

Salary Range
Less than $42,330 to $124,520 or more (all psychologists)

Number of Jobs
About 166,600 jobs in 2016 (all psychologists)

Future Job Outlook
Better than average

such as athlete performance and well-being, developmental and social aspects of sports, and common issues such as the tendency to emphasize performance outcomes over individual athletes' well-being. In their research and practice, sport psychologists draw from studies in the fields of psychology, sport science, and medicine.

While jobs for sport psychologists were not advertised back in 1937, the Chicago Cubs baseball team tried an innovative strategy that year. Psychologist Coleman Griffith was hired to help the team improve its performance by adding psychological techniques and principles to its physical training and performance regimen. Sport psychology, then, has existed in practice (if not by name) for close to a century. Nevertheless, within professional psychology it is a relatively new and recently fast-growing official specialization. In 2003 the APA first recognized sport psychology as an official proficiency (approved knowledge or skill area) for professional psychologists. Jobs for sport psychologists may involve research, teaching, clinical work and/or counseling, or a combination of these activities. Sport psychologists who teach at colleges and universities also conduct research about how sports participation affects motivation, psychological development, emotional health, and other related areas. Based on their original research, they write and publish articles in academic journals. As professors, they develop and teach courses, advise students, and fulfill administrative responsibilities. Some professors also work with athletes and teams on campus in a counseling or consulting role.

Sport psychologists might use cognitive and behavioral skills training in counseling, clinical interventions, consultations, and training. They help athletes, coaches, support staff, officials, and other sports participants improve their performance and/or overcome psychological barriers, perform consistently, and reach their full potential in sports. To do so, sport psychologists use approaches that include relaxation and anxiety management techniques, concentration strategies, and visualization exercises.

Sport psychologist John F. Murray has worked with NFL players, Wimbledon tennis stars, and Olympic athletes. He teaches them how to use mental rituals that help them calmly focus right before an important shot or play. Murray observes in an interview with *Psychology Today*, "The time between points in tennis, shots in golf, or plays in football, may be as important to master as the playing time. The pre-action ritual replaces distracted thinking with something constructive." Sport psychologists like Murray also help athletes prepare for the intense demands of training and competition with techniques to enhance goal setting, removal of mental obstacles, communication, and team building.

Some clinical sport psychologists provide therapy for clients with mental health challenges that impede their performance in or are related to their participation in sports. These may include depression, eating disorders, suicidal thoughts, anxiety disorders, and other conditions. These professionals provide counseling regarding a variety of job-related problems, such as concussion-related mental health issues, isolation, and physical pain management related to injury-related rehabilitation. They provide support and strategies related to substance abuse, sexual identity issues, and burnout from overtraining.

In addition to working with adult athletes, many sport psychologists are hired to work with children and coaches. Youth and their families seek counseling from sport psychologists for bullying or hazing, participation anxiety, self-confidence, and maintaining a healthy balance between sports and school. Coaches work with sport psychologists to gain professional support related to team building, motivation, leadership skills and talent development, and/or identification and prevention of psychological problems affecting players.

Demand for sport psychologists extends throughout the sports industry. Sport psychologist Jeremy Snape, who works with England's rugby union team, comments in the *Guardian*, "when people reach the very top we often hear that it was their mental game that led to their success. With so many world champions speaking positively about their mindset training now it has created a new drive for people to find out what they could achieve." Increasingly, both athletes and coaches are becoming aware that psychological skills and techniques combine with physical performance to contribute to success in sports, and this bodes well for future sport psychologists.

How Do You Become a Sport Psychologist?

Education

Psychologists must have a doctoral degree in psychology. The PhD, a research-oriented degree that requires a dissertation, is normally required for a teaching or research position at a college or university and for high-level consulting. Sport psychologists may practice with the PsyD degree, which emphasizes practical work and exams rather than research and a dissertation. Undergraduates can begin to prepare by majoring in psychology, kinesiology, or both.

Because it is a relatively new specialty, only a few colleges and universities offer a graduate program in sport psychology. As a result, some sport psychologists enroll in a regular doctoral program in psychology and take additional courses in kinesiology, sports medicine, biomechanics, physiology, business, and marketing. Others enroll in physical education or sport sciences doctoral programs and take supplemental psychology course work, including abnormal psychology, principles of counseling, psychopathology, personality, and social psychology.

Certification and Licensing

Certification is usually required for practicing psychologists who plan to work in hospitals or clinics. The American Board of Professional Psychology offers certification for all specialties within professional psychology. The Association for Applied Sport Psychology also offers an alternative certification program for candidates with a master's or doctoral degree in psychology, sport science, or a related field. This certification confers the title of mental performance consultant, which is not technically the same as a sport psychologist.

To use the titles psychologist or sport psychologist, a license is required. Practicing psychologists take the licensing Examination for Professional Practice in Psychology. Most states require ongoing education in order to retain the license. Specific laws regarding psychologist licenses vary depending on the state and employer or position.

Internships

Most psychologist jobs (as well as licensing boards) require an internship and supervised experience at the postgraduate level. Specific requirements vary by state. Graduate degree programs in psychology usually include a yearlong internship and residency. Psychology graduate students may also work as psychological assistants under a psychologist's supervision.

Some colleges or universities offer psychology internships, and the Association for Applied Sport Psychology offers a program that matches students and mentors. Many graduate students who are unable to find internship opportunities specifically related to sport psychology complete other types of internships in clinical psychology.

Skills and Personality

Sport psychologists should be caring and compassionate, with excellent communication and interpersonal skills. They should be committed to ethical responsibility and able to keep sensitive information confidential. It is helpful to have a knack for analyzing information and arriving at conclusions. Since graduate work is required and treatment is based on the results of research in the field, the best candidates will enjoy research and demonstrate the ability to relate scientific information to practical applications. It is helpful to have personal experience with or knowledge of sports.

On the Job

Employers

There are many different types of employment settings for sport psychologists. Some of these include hospitals and clinics, rehabilitation centers, fitness centers, high schools, colleges and universities, professional sports programs and teams, and private practice. Many professional athletes hire sport psychologists and pay them directly. Sport psychologists are sometimes hired by parents to work with youth athletes, and they develop resources for coaches of youth sports.

Some sport psychologists counsel athletes to help them overcome psychological barriers and other problems that impede athletic performance. Others work in research settings or teach.

The US Olympic Committee maintains a team of board-certified psychologists who work with athletes to prepare them for the intense demands of Olympic competition. To be included on the US Olympic Committee Sport Psychology and Mental Training Registry of professionals approved to work with Olympic and national teams, requirements include a doctoral degree, a Certified Consultant degree from the Association for Applied Sport Psychology, and membership in the APA.

Working Conditions

Professors of sport psychology work in offices and classrooms at universities. They may conduct research and/or counsel athletes at sporting events, practices, and training.

Some applied psychologists work full time, usually 9:00 a.m. to 5:00 p.m., for clinics or organizations. According to the APA, however, full-time jobs are limited, so many sport psychologists work part-time or combine their specialty with other types of psychology work. Sport psychologists in private practice may set their own work hours, as long as they are available as needed to clients. Sometimes this means working unusual hours. Work settings vary depending on the client and position. Some sport psychologists who work with a team must also travel with the team.

Earnings

Median annual pay for all psychologists (including sport psychologists) in 2017 was $77,030, according to the Bureau of Labor Statistics (BLS). Pay ranges from less than $42,330 to over $124,520. Sport psychologists working at university athletic departments are likely to earn between $60,000 and $80,000 a year, according to an article on the APA website.

Opportunities for Advancement

Sport psychologists often start out working for university athletic departments. Some advance to work with national sports teams, well-known athlete clients, or even an Olympic team. Sport psychologists who work as professors at universities advance through promotions and tenure, according to the criteria at their place of employment.

What Is the Future Outlook for Sport Psychologists?

According to the BLS, the future outlook for psychologists is a faster-than-average job growth of 14 percent through 2026. Data is not available regarding the projected outlook for sport psychologists as a group, but sport psychology is considered by the APA to be a "hot career." An article on the APA website notes that industry leaders see a hopeful future for those interested in the job. In that article, Scott Goldman, director of clinical and sport psychology at the University of Arizona, indicates the strength of the field, stating that "at least 20 NCAA Division I universities have a sport psychologist on staff and another 70 to 100 contract with outside specialists." The American Kinesiology Association similarly notes in *Careers in Sports, Fitness, and Exercise* that the demand for sport psychologists is growing and expanding across different sectors, from professional and collegiate athletes to youth and coaches involved in recreational sports. With increased participation in sports at various levels has come growing recognition of the value of mental skills training.

Find Out More

American Board of Professional Psychology (ABPP)
600 Market St., Suite 201
Chapel Hill, NC 27516
website: www.abpp.org

The ABPP is the organization that oversees specialty board certification for professional psychologists in areas such as clinical, counseling, school, rehabilitation, and more.

APA Division 47: Society for Sport, Exercise, and Performance Psychology
American Psychological Association
750 First St. NE
Washington, DC 20002
website: www.apadivisions.org/division-47

Division 47 is the branch of the APA that represents and provides resources for exercise and sport psychology. Its website offers a wealth of up-to-date information in areas including education and training standards, books and journals, conference information, and training webinars on important topics related to sport psychology.

Association for Applied Sport Psychology
8365 Keystone Crossing, Suite 107
Indianapolis, IN 46240
website: www.appliedsportpsych.org

This group is an international professional organization for sport psychologists. It offers a certification program, publishes journals and case studies, operates an annual conference, and provides resources related to the profession, including a career center.

**Association of State and Provincial
Psychology Boards (ASPPB)**
215 Market Rd.
Tyrone, GA 30290
website: www.asppb.net

The ASPPB oversees and standardizes certification and licensing for psychologists in the United States and Canada. It develops the licensing Examination for Professional Practice in Psychology and provides information about licensing requirements in different states.

**North American Society for the Psychology
of Sport and Physical Activity (NASPSPA)**
website: www.naspspa.com

The NASPSPA is a membership organization for anyone interested in motor behavior and/or sport and exercise psychology. Half of its members are graduate students. The organization sponsors awards for faculty and graduate students and posts job listings on its website.

Physical Education Teacher

At a Glance

Physical Education Teacher

Minimum Educational Requirements
Bachelor's degree

Personal Qualities
Patient, enthusiastic, outgoing, enjoys sports and working with youth and adolescents

Certification and Licensing
Physical education teaching certification required

Working Conditions
Indoor and outdoor venues, school hours and beyond, class sizes vary

Salary Range
About $37,340 to $95,380 (all teachers, a category that includes PE teachers)

Number of Jobs
About 1.5 million (all kindergarten and elementary school teachers); 630,300 (all middle school teachers); 1 million (all high school teachers); 1.3 million (all postsecondary teachers)

Future Job Outlook
About average

What Does a Physical Education Teacher Do?

When researchers with Children's Hospital of Eastern Ontario and the University of North Dakota compared the physical fitness testing results of over 1 million children in fifty nations in 2016, US children (ages nine through seventeen) ranked near the bottom, at number forty-seven. What is more, according to a report by the Centers for Disease Control and Prevention, childhood obesity rates have more than tripled since the 1970s, with almost 20 percent of children ages six to nineteen considered obese. In recent years broad initiatives to help American kids eat right and get fit include former First Lady Michelle Obama's Let's Move! program and the Aspen Institute's Project Play. In schools across America, physical education teachers make a difference every day, student by student, in the effort to promote a higher level of physical activity and health among America's youth.

Physical education teachers (or PE teachers for short) are education professionals who teach about sports, exercise and fitness, nutrition, and physical health in schools ranging from preschool to college. They share with all teachers the primary responsibilities of developing curriculum, planning lessons, and delivering instruction to students.

When a new PE teacher starts a job, the school typically presents him or her with a written curriculum guide that details specific responsibilities for instructing all students by grade level. In public schools, the curriculum must support local, state, and national health and fitness standards for youth physical education. Some PE teachers create and revise PE curriculum at their schools.

In their daily lessons, PE teachers plan and deliver activities, drills, and games for students that address skills and competencies needed by students at each grade level. They guide students of all ability levels, sometimes including students with disabilities, to set and reach fitness and performance goals. They provide feedback and motivation to help students improve, to teach sports games and associated rules and strategies, and to instruct students in motor skill development, strength, and agility.

Some students do not enjoy PE class. To motivate all students, many PE teachers develop unique approaches for their lesson plans. For example, PE teacher Martine Carr, who teaches elementary school students at Annunciation Orthodox School in Houston, Texas, encourages kids to complete laps around the track by recording their distances as "travel miles" to various imagined world destinations. She explains in her "Best Practice" post on the physical education website PE Central:

> Every Wednesday at our school is travel day in P.E. class. Students come to the travel field . . . to walk, jog, or run as many laps as they can. . . . The lap scores are calculated into mileage and recorded on a map in the P.E. hall at school. The first year we ran around the United States traveling to all the State capitals. . . . On our last travel day we

traveled to a pool to swim to Hawaii and have a luau. . . . We have traveled to Europe, South America and the past two years have been spent walking and jogging through Africa.

While these types of creative approaches enable PE teachers to introduce their own ideas in lesson plans, in most states, PE teachers must also oversee and record results of mandatory physical performance tests. They also document student progress and assign report card grades.

Lesson content varies depending on the age level of the students. The small number of PE teachers who work in preschools generally provide young children with their first exposure to basic motor skills and movement. PE teachers in elementary schools focus on coordination, teamwork and sportsmanship skills, and appropriate behavior (such as not being a sore loser). In an interview posted on the National Education Association website, PE teacher Jen Roddel, who works at Central Elementary School in Ferndale, Washington, emphasizes this important part of her job: "I teach them how to make decisions that impact their bodies and their lives. I teach them that winning isn't everything and losing can be a learning experience. I teach them how to treat human beings with fairness and thoughtfulness. I teach them that not everyone gets to 'win.'"

In addition to continued sportsmanship lessons, at the middle and high school levels, PE classes include traditional sports (baseball, soccer, basketball, and so on), as well as games such as Capture the Flag and other physical activities, including dance, jumping rope, yoga, and aerobics. In colleges and universities, PE teachers may be assigned to teach required courses and electives in a wide variety of team and individual sports classes for PE credit, as well as aerobics, dance, and exercise classes. Many high school and college PE teachers work with coaches to identify strong players for school sports teams. At colleges where team sports are strong, PE teachers may also refer talented athletes to scouts or professional teams.

In all types of schools and employment settings, PE teachers must keep abreast of changing state and local standards and school expectations around physical fitness. It is also important for them to be aware of new technology that improves PE instruction, such as fitness apps, activity trackers, and heart rate monitors. In addition to their instructional duties, many PE teachers are responsible for keeping the gym and athletic facilities in good condition and for completing accident reports and insurance forms. They also typically attend faculty meetings and in-service workshops and help the school with special events.

How Do You Become a Physical Education Teacher?

Education

Taking science classes and participating in physical education and sports will help high school students prepare for a career in physical education before college. A bachelor's degree is required to become a PE teacher. Appropriate college majors include health and physical education, nutrition science, and kinesiology. To qualify for a teaching credential, PE teachers usually complete a separate teacher education program that includes supervised student teaching. Some PE teachers earn master's and doctoral degrees and go on to teach in colleges or universities.

Certification and Licensing

Teachers in public schools must be certified with a teaching credential from the board of education in their state of employment. A background check is also required. PE teachers require a single-subject physical education credential for kindergarten through twelfth-grade teaching. In many states, teachers must enroll in continuing education courses to keep their certification current. Some, but not all, states offer an adapted physical education certificate for teachers who are already certified to teach physical education and have also completed course work and supervised experience providing instruction to students with disabilities. Most, but not all, private and/or parochial schools require certification for teachers of physical education. Also, many schools require first aid and cardiopulmonary resuscitation certifications.

While state certification requirements vary, most states have reciprocal agreements that enable teachers who are certified in one state to also teach in another. To learn about certification requirements in a particular state, job seekers should contact the state's board of education.

Volunteer Work and Internships

Some of the many opportunities that provide experience for future PE teachers include working as counselors in summer camps, teaching or assisting at recreation centers, teaching private sports lessons, and helping out in recreational athletic programs. Recreational baseball and soccer leagues often offer children and adolescents a variety of volunteer jobs.

Skills and Personality

PE teachers should be enthusiastic and outgoing, and they should enjoy working with young people and leading activities. While PE teachers work with other faculty and staff members, the majority of their time is spent with children and adolescents. It is not uncommon for PE teachers to encounter and deal with student behavior problems, so patience and effective leadership abilities are important. PE teachers should be good communicators, effective mentors, and team players, because they work with a broad range of teachers, staff, and students throughout the workday. Of course, they should have a passion for physical activities and sports and a strong desire to lead others.

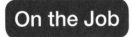

On the Job

Employers

Most PE teachers work in public K–12 schools, but jobs are also available in private schools and a small number of preschools. Some PE teachers work in colleges and universities.

Working Conditions

PE teachers work in indoor gymnasiums and outdoor recreation fields. They may wear comfortable (but professional) sports clothing to work. The workday and hours vary depending on the school assignment. Many elementary school physical education teachers work at more than one school and must travel between teaching periods. Some physical education teachers provide daily instruction to multiple classes, while others see students only one or two times a week. In addition to teaching during normal school hours, PE teachers may attend curriculum and lesson planning meetings, coach sports teams, and perform administrative work after school. Like students, PE teachers normally enjoy a summer vacation period.

Earnings

Earnings for PE teachers depend on the type of employer. According to the National Education Association, the average starting salary for all public school teachers in 2016–2017 was $38,617. Salaries vary from state to state and from school district to school district. The highest starting salaries were earned in Washington, DC ($51,359), and the lowest in Montana ($30,036). Annual salary ranges for all teachers (including physical education and other subjects) nationwide in 2016–2017 were about $39,080 to $95,380 (high school teachers), $38,540 to $91,670 (middle school teachers), and $37,340 to $92,770 (elementary school teachers, not including special education teachers). On average, private school teachers earn less than public school teachers.

Opportunities for Advancement

PE teachers working in K–12 schools may be promoted to jobs such as athletic director, assistant athletic director, or coaching director. Teachers also advance by moving from a small school to a higher-paying job at a larger school. However, teachers who remain at the same school for a prescribed number of years earn tenure, which provides job security. Some physical education teachers earn master's or doctoral degrees and, after experience teaching in elementary, middle, or high school, go on to work in colleges and universities. College PE teachers advance by moving to a larger or more prestigious college or to a job as department head or athletic director. Teacher salaries increase with additional educational credits or degrees beyond the bachelor's degree.

What Is the Future Outlook for Physical Education Teachers?

The Bureau of Labor Statistics (BLS) does not collect statistics for physical education teachers as a group. However, it predicts 8 percent growth (about average) for both middle school and high school teacher jobs through 2026. The growth rate for elementary school jobs (7 percent) is similar. The BLS predicts a faster-than-average growth rate of 15 percent for postsecondary teachers (again, in all teacher specialty areas) through 2026.

Find Out More

National Education Association (NEA)
1201 Sixteenth St. NW
Washington, DC 20036
website: www.nea.org

The NEA is a very large organization that represents public school teachers, college and university faculty and staff, and college students who intend to become teachers. The organization provides teaching-related resources and seeks to influence laws and policies related to education in America.

PE Central
PE Central/Mark Manross
2516 Blossom Trail W.
Blacksburg, VA 24060
website: www.pecentral.org

This website provides extensive resources to support the work of professionals in health and physical education. It is a clearinghouse for assessments, lesson plans and ideas, examples of best practices, videos, and online professional development classes.

PEteacherEDU.org
website: www.peteacheredu.org

This organization provides state-by-state information about the process of becoming a certified PE teacher, as well as how to maintain and upgrade a teaching license.

SHAPE America—Society of Health and Physical Educators
1900 Association Dr.
Reston, VA 20191
website: www.shapeamerica.org

This membership organization creates guidelines and standards for K–12 health and physical fitness that are used by schools across America. Its website offers numerous resources and publications for PE teachers, as well as information about events and conferences.

Interview with a Sport Psychologist

Shira Oretzky is a licensed clinical psychologist and sport psychologist. She is a faculty member at San Diego State University, where she works with NCAA Division I athletes, and she has a private practice in La Jolla, California. She has worked as a sport psychologist for ten years. She answered questions about her career by e-mail.

Q: Why did you become a sport psychologist?
A: Sports have always been an integral part of my life. As a kid I was a competitive gymnast and later went on to play volleyball and soccer. Sports were key in my development, and I saw how they have positively shaped others.

From a young age, I was also intrigued by psychology and the mind. After college, I went on to graduate school to get a PhD. in clinical psychology. My dissertation research looked at how yoga can improve depression, anxiety and physical symptoms in young adults. My approach to practice was influenced by seeing first-hand the positive implications of how combined treatment of mind and body can significantly improve an individual's overall health and well-being. After graduate school I went on to complete a proficiency in Sport Psychology, honing my psychological knowledge and clinical skills to address the optimal performance and well-being of athletes as well as developmental and social aspects of sports.

Being a sport psychologist was a perfect fit. It incorporates two things that I am passionate about: sports and psychology.

Q: Can you describe your typical workday?

A: I work as a faculty psychologist at San Diego State University, where I am the liaison to Athletics. I also have a sport psychology practice where I do private consulting with individual athletes, teams, and organizations.

At the University, the majority of a typical day is spent in individual meetings with student-athletes to address sport- or performance-related concerns and to develop skills and techniques for enhancing peak performance. I talk with student-athletes about a variety of challenges they experience. These include managing the pressures of performing at a high level, adjusting to college, relationships with others, clinical mental health issues like depression or anxiety, recovering from injuries, and navigating the transition from college sports to either playing professionally or an alternative career path. A typical day often involves phone calls with Athletic Medicine Doctors, Athletic Trainers, Athletic Academic Advisors, and other key supports in the athlete's life. We work together as a team to best support the athlete. Additionally, I regularly work on programming educational workshops that teach sport psychology skills and address mental wellness topics, for both athlete seminars and teams.

Q: What do you like most about your job?

A: I love working with athletes. Their passion, strength, and determination to succeed continually inspires me and it's a pleasure to have the opportunity to help them reach their potential.

My job is extremely rewarding. I love to sit one-on-one with athletes and hear about their life stories, career paths, and future goals and aspirations. When I see an athlete thriving in his or her sport and life after working through mental blocks, overcoming fears, or building confidence, I find it quite gratifying.

Q: What do you like least about your job?

A: The challenging part of my job has been to increase awareness of the importance of athlete mental wellness. In the past, there has been a stigma associated with mental health, especially in the sports culture. The encouraging part is that strides are being made. As professional and college athletes, the NCAA, and sport organizations continue to open up the dialogue around this area, it is exciting to be in this field!

Q: What personal qualities do you find most valuable for this type of work?

A: Good interpersonal skills go a long way in this field. Being able to build positive relationships, communicate effectively, and offer genuine care about the well-being of your clients are all very important. Having an athletic background yourself with experience competing in sports is an invaluable asset to this type of work and helps to establish credibility and to be seen as relatable by athletes. Being creative and having the ability to think outside the box are also helpful. Flexibility and adaptability are key. It is important to be able to build rapport easily with athletes from diverse backgrounds and to be prepared to work with a variety of team and organizational cultures.

Q: What is the best way to prepare for this type of job?

A: Education, experience, and professional connections are key. Take courses in psychology, exercise science, and sport and exercise psychology to help determine your interest in this area. Get involved in opportunities like research or volunteer coaching. Join professional organizations such as the Association for Applied Sport Psychology and the American Psychological Association, Division 47 and attend their annual conferences. Talk to professionals in the field to learn about their career paths and internship opportunities.

Q: What other advice do you have for students who might be interested in this career?

A: This is an excellent time to enter the field of sport psychology because it is expanding. The career path is not clearly defined, which might require a student to be creative in putting together an educational training and applied experience. With a passion for the field, ambition, and a strong work ethic there is great opportunity to build an exciting career for yourself. The work is stimulating, no two days are the same, and the rewards of helping athletes to truly reach their potential are tremendously fulfilling.

Other Jobs in Sports

Equipment manager
eSports game designer
eSports professional player
eSports shoutcaster/host
Fantasy sports website
  designer
Fitness instructor
Mascot
Music supervisor/disc jockey
Physical therapist
Public relations manager
Recreational center director
Recreational therapist
Scoreboard operator
Scout
Sports accountant
Sports account executive
Sports agent

Sports attorney
Sports camp counselor
Sports camp director
Sports dietitian
Sports event coordinator
Sports facility manager
Sports media specialist
Sports medicine physician
Sports photographer
Sports public relations director
Statistical analyst
Strength and agility coach
Team general manager
Team owner
Team promotions director
Team publicist
Team webmaster
Vendor

Editor's Note: The US Department of Labor's Bureau of Labor Statistics provides information about hundreds of occupations. The agency's *Occupational Outlook Handbook* describes what these jobs entail, the work environment, education and skill requirements, pay, future outlook, and more. The *Occupational Outlook Handbook* may be accessed online at www.bls.gov/ooh.

Index